CURIOUS Questions and Answers About...

Clever Inventors

Words by Sue Nicholson
Illustrations by Flavio Remonetti

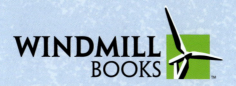

Are All Inventions New?

Some are, but usually inventors look at something that already exists then change it, to make it even better.

What is an inventor?

Anyone who designs or builds something new is called an inventor. Some people have many ideas; others have just one brilliant idea.

In the 1870s, James Bedford Elliott took the big wheel off the penny farthing to create a unicycle.

It's dangerous being so high up. What if the seat was lower and I added a chain?

1871 – Ariel "penny farthing" by James Starley

1885 – Rover "safety bicycle" by John Starley

Modern bikes have almost the same design as the Rover!

Which Invention Lit Up the World?

After the discovery of fire, ancient humans invented little oil-burning lamps to see in the dark. They also made tools, mirrors, and wheels.

Hand axes chipped from flint were used almost two million years ago.

Oil lamp

The earliest mirrors were made 8,000 years ago out of polished black glassy rock.

People living long ago also invented wheels, and shaped clay into pots. Later they made carts.

Who started scribbling?

People came up with different ways of writing all around the world.

The ancient Sumerians (4500–1900 BCE) invented a way of writing, called cuneiform.

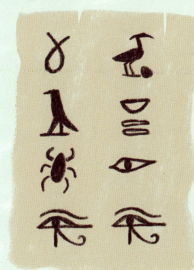

The ancient Egyptians (around 3100 BCE) wrote in little pictures, called hieroglyphs.

The Ancient Chinese (around 1250 BCE) wrote in characters called Hanzi.

The Phoenicians, ancient Greeks, and ancient Romans (between 1500 BCE and 750 BCE) wrote in an alphabet, which records the sound of speech.

How did millions of people end up with books?

Johannes Gutenberg's book printing press of the 1400s made books easier to make and cheaper to buy. Before this, books had to be copied out by hand, which took too long.

Today we can use an e-reader to read books. The first ones were created in the 1990s.

A screw presses paper onto moveable metal letters.

The letters are covered with ink and make an exact copy each time.

Did You Know?

In the 1800s, **Josephine Cochran** invented the dishwasher. Big dishwashers were first used by hotels and restaurants.

Emojis were created in 1999 by **Shigetaka Kurita**. The first emojis all had just 144 pixels (little squares of data).

Smaller dishwashers didn't make it into people's homes until the 1950s.

A new fizzy drink was made by **Dr John Pemberton** in his yard in 1886. He sold it as a "brain tonic" and it became the world-famous Coca Cola.

Alan Turing was an amazing mathematician who worked for the British government during World War II as a code-breaker.

Alan Turing's bomb code-breaking machine

American president **Theodore Roosevelt Jr.** was also known as Teddy. He hadn't wanted to shoot a real bear on a hunting trip and a toymaker made a stuffed bear of him and named it "Teddy's bear."

The 24-hour clock for the whole world was devised by **Sandford Fleming** in 1876, later called "Cosmic Time."

Denim jeans were created by **Jacob W. Davis** and **Levi Strauss** in the 1870s for goldminers, who needed hard-wearing clothes.

Play-Doh, invented by the **McVicker** family in the 1930s, started out as something to clean soot off wallpaper!

John Logie Baird's first attempt at creating a television in 1923 was made using a hat box, knitting needles, and bicycle lamps!

9

Who Was Ahead of His Time?

Leonardo da Vinci was one of the world's cleverest inventors. He lived over 500 years ago, but he came up with futuristic ideas for all kinds of things long before people knew how to build them.

A winged flying machine.

I was interested in space, flight, how bodies work, science, painting, mathematics, and sculpture.

A battle tank covered with metal plates, which had a turret on top to fire weapons through.

A machine with a turning spiral at the top and blades to power it into the air.

How did da Vinci record his ideas?

Put a mirror here

Leonardo used mirror writing in his notebooks — maybe so other people didn't steal his clever ideas!

Who else had awesome, ancient ideas?

Archimedes (287–212 BCE) invented a huge wooden screw to raise water from rivers.

Chinese inventor **Zhang Heng** devised a way to detect distant earthquakes in 132 AD.

Eight ornate dragons

Eight open-mouthed toads

Bronze urn with swinging pendulum inside

The dragons, each with a copper ball, faced different directions. When a tremor was felt, the pendulum swung and a ball from the direction of the tremor dropped down to the toad.

A revolving crane to pick up heavy loads.

Engineer **Ismail Al-Jazari** (1136–1206) invented intricate clocks, locks, and all sorts of mechanical toys.

Who Got Us Moving?

Early transportation inventions were often created by people working alone. Nowadays, entire teams of people work together to develop ideas.

Wernher von Braun and his team at NASA designed the Saturn V rockets in the 1960s, which took astronauts to the Moon.

Orville and Wilbur Wright flew the first plane in 1903.

How are planes getting greener?

Clever inventors are experimenting with solar-powered planes to make air transportation cleaner and better for the environment.

Solar Impulse 2

Robert Goddard made and launched the first liquid-fueled rocket from a farm in Massachusetts in 1926.

I did! I'm Frank Searle. In 1909, I designed the first London double-decker bus.

The PlanetSolar built by the Knierim shipyard, was the first solar-powered boat to sail around the world between 2010 and 2012.

I did, in 1885! I'm Karl Benz. My car had three wheels and could only travel at 10 miles (16 km) an hour!

Who had a wheelie good idea?

How did we learn to float a boat?

Early people worked out how to carve simple boats from tree trunks. Later, people built boats with sails that could be pushed by the wind.

13

How Many?

5,127 prototypes made by inventor **James Dyson** before he got his new bagless vacuum cleaner just right.

748,626 U.S. patent number of "The Landlord's Game," also known as "Monopoly," invented by **Lizzie J. Magie** in 1904.

Fugaku, one of the world's fastest supercomputers can work at **442 quadrillion** (one thousand trillion) calculations a second.

Today, there are over 100 colors of crayon with names like Robin's Egg Blue and Jazzberry Jam.

Famous U.S. inventor, **Thomas Edison**, said, "Genius is **1** percent inspiration, **99** percent perspiration."

8 colors in the first-ever box of Crayola crayons, invented by **Edwin Binney** and **C. Harold Smith** in 1903.

200 miles an hour. Top speed of Japanese Shinkansen "bullet trains" designed by **Hideo Shima** and his team of engineers in 1964.

30 miles an hour.

Top speed of the Rocket, one of the world's first-ever steam locomotives, invented by **George Stephenson** in 1829.

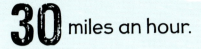

355 inventions patented by **Alfred Nobel**, including one for dynamite. He requested the Nobel Prize be set up in his name in 1896.

Bill Gates, chairman of Microsoft Corporation, bought one of Leonardo da Vinci's surviving notebooks, in 1994 for...

$30 million

Gymnast **George Nissen** was **16** when he invented the trampoline in the 1930s.

Who Was a Bright Spark?

American inventor **Benjamin Franklin** flew a kite into a storm in 1752 to see whether electrical energy could be conducted. Many inventors then experimented with electricity as a usable power source.

Alessandro Volta (1745–1827) created the first electric battery.

My kite had a metal key attached to it and a wet string to conduct the "electric fire" of the lightning.

Don't try this at home!

Humphry Davy (1778–1829) worked out how an electrical current could create light.

Michael Faraday (1791–1867) made the first electro-magnetic generator, turning movement into power.

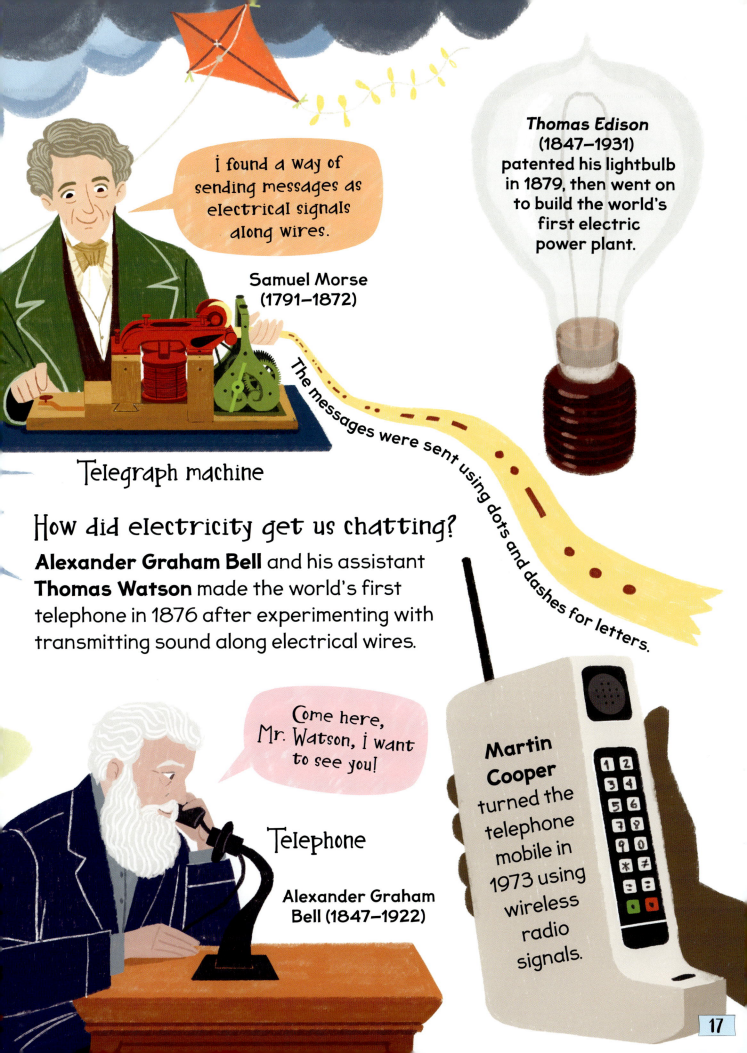

Which Inventions Have Saved Lives?

When a pandemic (a worldwide disease) was declared in March 2020, the Covid-19 vaccine was created, developed, and tested in a matter of months. It has saved millions of lives.

The first microscope was created in the 1600s to better understand disease. Microbiology is the study of microscopic organisms.

As technology improved, scientists could begin to see how tiny organisms like viruses and bacteria could cause illnesses and disease.

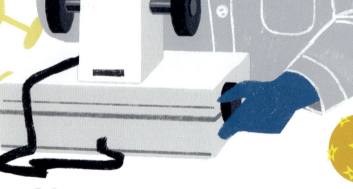

Who has helped athletes run like cheetahs?

Van Phillips, who lost one of his legs, is the inventor of Flex-Foot prosthetic limbs. The Flex-Foot Cheetah has a carbon-fiber blade to help athletes run fast.

What helps to see inside our bodies?

X-rays are used to look inside us to check for lumps, bumps, and broken bones. **Wilhelm Röntgen** took the first-ever X-ray in 1895 of his wife's hand.

Adhesive bandages were created in 1921 by Earle Dickson for his wife, who kept cutting her fingers when cooking.

Plaster cast

Blade flexes on impact with the ground

When was the first plaster cast?

Long ago, people used wooden splints and other methods to set broken bones. During World War I, **Anne Acheson** developed a way of using plaster of Paris to help set broken bones in a cast. This kind of plaster cast is still used today.

19

Would You Rather?

Meet **Leonardo da Vinci** or...

...**Markus Persson**, the creator of Minecraft?

Invent a pair of winged hover **boots** or a **plane** with flapping wings?

Take a trip on the **fastest train** in the world or...

...ride an early '**penny farthing**'?

Create a new kind of **chocolate bar** like Francis Fry or a new kind of **breakfast cereal** like Joseph Kellogg?

The Fry family sold drinking chocolate, but **Francis Fry** was the first person to make chocolate into a solid bar in 1847.

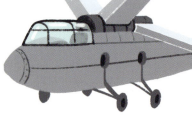

Who Was the Father of the Computer?

In the 1830s, **Charles Babbage** designed two clever computing machines to store and process numbers. His friend, **Ada Lovelace**, wrote the first computing code to one of his machines.

I didn't get around to completing my computing machines, but if I had, one of them might have looked a bit like this...

Babbage's proposed Analytical Engine is considered to be the first-ever computer

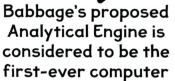

Charles Babbage (1791–1871)

In the 1940s an enormous electric computer called ENIAC was built. Today, the whole processing power and speed of ENIAC can fit onto one tiny silicon chip!

When were supercomputers invented?

Seymour Cray built the first superfast supercomputer in 1976. It was giant, and it got so hot it had to have a special cooling system to stop it from melting.

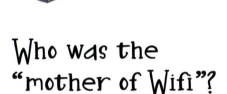

Who was the "mother of Wifi"?

Hedy Lamarr was a famous Hollywood actress, but her real love was inventing. During World War II she invented a type of frequency-hopping technology.

My invention became the basis for today's Wifi and Bluetooth!

How do computers talk to each other?

Tim Berners-Lee created a universal computing language known as hypertext markup language (HTML) in 1989. It was the beginning of the World Wide Web and he gave his invention to the world for free, without taking out any patents.

Are Things Ever Invented by Accident?

Once set in motion, the Slinky transfers energy along its length to allow it to "walk."

Yes! When naval engineer **Richard James** dropped a spring he was working with in 1943, he was stunned to see it "walk" down a stack of books onto the floor. Soon, he'd invented Slinky toys!

Frank Epperson (1894–1983)

When I was 11, I created the first ice pop. I left my drink outside overnight with a stirring stick in it. In the morning, it had frozen!

Who had a blast with water?

Space engineer **Lonnie Johnson** did! He came up with the idea for a Super Soaker water gun in 1989 when he accidentally fired water across his bathroom while doing an experiment for a new space mission.

Whose sticky glue idea came unstuck?
In 1968, **Spencer Silver** was trying to invent a new, extra-strong glue, but it just wasn't sticky, so he gave up...

...A few years later, **Arthur Fry** used Silver's accidental invention of non-sticky glue to make reusable bookmarks or "post-it" notes.

Which tasty cereal was made by mistake?

The Kellogg brothers tried to make granola in 1898, but accidentally flaked wheat berries instead.

Then they tried flaking corn and invented a whole new breakfast cereal!

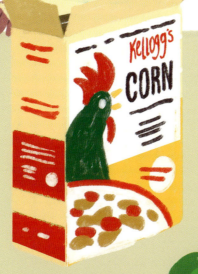

Lonnie Johnson (b. 1949)

Whose Inventions Are Helping Our Planet?

As Earth is so polluted by plastic litter and dirty gases, clever inventors are now busy trying to create clean energy and tidy up the mess we've made.

What kind of snake is cleaning our oceans?

A long, snake-like floating barrier was invented by **Boyan Slat** in 2017. Called the Ocean Cleanup system, the "snake" gathers up plastic and other pollution floating in our oceans, so it can be recycled.

A 10-foot (3 m) skirt beneath the surface lets marine life pass through

The Ocean Cleanup system is busy tackling the Great Pacific Garbage Patch — a mass of floating trash twice the size of France.

Support vessel

Whose wings are inspiring new inventions?

Scientists have discovered tiny spaced holes on the wings of the swallowtail butterfly. Inventors are using this discovery to improve the design of solar cells.

Tiny holes scatter sunlight

In 2018 Fionn Ferreira found an environmentally safe way of using ferrofluid. This naturally magnetic liquid can remove microplastic particles from water.

Microplastic particles

My water purification invention won a national science prize when I was 14.

How can sunlight save lives?

When **Deepika Kurup** began visiting India with her family, she couldn't believe people were lining up for dirty water. At home in the U.S. in 2012 she began to work on an inexpensive way of purifying water using sunlight.

Can Kids Be Inventors?

Yes! Some incredible things have been thought up by people not much older than you. You could invent a device to help people, a new kind of fuel, or a way to make a favorite toy even better.

Be inquisitive, determined, and persistent like Richard. Use your imagination! Wonder "what if" and always ask LOTS of curious questions!

Richard Turere

A Kenyan Maasai herder, Richard Turere, was only 11 years old when he invented Lion Lights. He connected a string of lights to an old car battery to scare lions away from his tribe's cattle. Lion Lights are widely used across Kenya today.

Ruth Amos

Ruth invented the StairSteady, to help people up and down stairs, as part of a school project when she was 15. She now has a YouTube channel called "Kids Invent Stuff" where you can send ideas for her to build on camera!

Ann Makosinski

A friend told Ann that she'd failed a test because her family didn't have electricity for her to study at night. So, in 2013, Ann invented a flashlight powered by the heat from its user's hand.

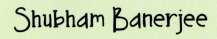

Shubham Banerjee

When he was 13 years old, Shubham invented a low-cost portable Braille printer, called the Braigo, using a Lego robotics kit.

Kylie Simonds

When ill with cancer in 2013, Kylie struggled to walk around with IV poles and wires. She invented an IV backpack for kids like her receiving chemotherapy or transfusions.

A Compendium of Questions

How did a plant inspire... ...some grippy stuff?

George de Mestral came up with the idea for Velcro in the 1950s, after examining the tiny burdock burrs caught in his dog's fur.

Why is Bluetooth called Bluetooth?

Invented in 1994 by **Jaap Haartsen**, Bluetooth links electronic devices without cables. It's named after Harald Bluetooth, the 10th century King of Denmark, famous for uniting Scandinavia.

Why is my pen called a Biro?

Lots of companies now make ballpoint pens, but **László Bíró** was the inventor who came up with a way of making ink flow smoothly from a tiny ball instead of a nib.

What was created because of a love of fish?

The aquarium! **Jeanne Villepreux-Power** was so fascinated by marine life, she found a better way to study it by inventing the aquarium in 1832.

Who was nicknamed King Pong?

Nolan Bushnell was given the nickname after inventing Pong, one of the first video games in 1972 — two players had to bounce a ball over a net.

Who wanted kids to "play well"?

Ole Kirk Christiansen's famous LEGO invention comes from two Danish words LEg GOdt, which mean "play well."

Whose feet have inspired ideas?

Mine! I'm a gecko and my feet are covered in millions of tiny hairs, inspiring the invention of super-sticky bandages.

Which invention is purr-fect?

The cat's eye! In 1934, **Percy Shaw** created little cat's eye reflectors that could be placed along roads, after almost crashing his car in the dark.

Published in 2026 by Windmill Books,
an Imprint of Rosen Publishing
2544 Clinton St.
Buffalo, NY 14224

First published in 2023 by Miles Kelly Publishing Ltd
Copyright © Miles Kelly Publishing Ltd 2023

Publishing Director   Belinda Gallagher
Creative Director   Jo Cowan
Editorial Director   Rosie Neave
Senior Editor   Fran Bromage
Designers   Simon Lee, Joe Jones, Karen Doughty
Image Manager   Liberty Newton
Production   Elizabeth Collins
Reprographics   Stephan Davis

Cataloging-in-Publication Data
Names: Nicholson, Sue, 1961-, author. | Remonetti, Flavio, illustrator.
Title: Clever inventors / by Sue Nicholson, illustrated by Flavio Remonetti.
Description: Buffalo, NY : Windmill Books, 2026. | Series: Curious questions and answers about...
Identifiers: ISBN 9781538398951 (pbk.) | ISBN 9781538398968 (library bound) | ISBN 9781538398975 (ebook)
Subjects: LCSH: Inventors--Juvenile literature. | Inventions--Juvenile fiction.
Classification: LCC T48.N534 2026 | DDC 600--dc23

All rights reserved.

No part of this book may be reproduced in any form without permission
in writing from the publisher, except by a reviewer.

Printed in the United States of America

CPSIA Compliance Information: Batch #CSWM26
For Further Information contact Rosen Publishing at 1-800-237-9932

Find us on